RAMTHA

The Children's View of Destiny and Purpose

Illustrated by the Children

JZK Publishing™
P.O. Box 1210
Yelm, Washington 98597
360·458·4771
800·347·0439
www.ramtha.com
greg@ramtha.com

The Children's View of Destiny and Purpose

by RAMTHA

Other titles by JZK Publishing™
The Mystery of Love (audio/book)
The Mystery of Love (CD/book)
A Beginner's Guide to Creating Reality
The Plane of Bliss

ISBN: 1-57873-005-8

Andrew

RAVEN

Derek

Benjamin

Children's Illustrations
by

Amiti Axe
Sam Axe
Raven Bridenthal
Andrew Busscher
Benjamin Mann
Lela McKenna
Nicole Newkirk
Derek Reger
Aria Reid
Paris Reid
Heather Shimono

Lela

nicole

Amiti

Sam

Paris

Heather

Aria

Story
by Ramtha

Book Design and Layout
by Gary Craig

Typesetting and Layout
by Laura Schuman

Proofreading
by Pat Richker

Words recorded March 7, 1996
by Debbie Christie

Hello? Ram to children. What I want you to understand about the story I'm going to tell you is that a lot of people have a great amount of difficulty trying to figure out how we got here and what we came out of.

Now the Void behind all of this didn't even have a face, didn't even have arms or hands or fingers, and it was quite lonely since it was the only thing around. It really wasn't a thing at all. It was nothing.

So one day it realized it was nothing. So when it realized it was nothing, at the point that it realized that, this big sun broke through in the middle of one vast nothing. It was ablaze.

Now today if you were to see that in your cosmology it would look like a large nebuli exploding, but the sun that appeared was actually the Void needing a face.

So the great face of the Void is the sun. So now suddenly this sun appeared in the midst of nothing and it was a happy sort of entity.

Notice it has a big smile on its face.

Well, we think this happened about Tuesday morning at 9:30 a.m. when this entity actually appeared. So what happened is that then the Void or creation finally got the face and the face looked like a radiating sun. And this sun was given a very important order.

The sun said, "I'm supposed to create everything. I'm supposed to have a very good time except I don't know what a good time is. But I'm supposed to have it and I get to do anything and everything that I want to do."

And so when the sun realized it got to do anything and everything it wanted to do, it also realized it was alone. Imagine getting to do everything when nothing existed; furthermore, getting to have fun when there was no such thing and there was no one to have fun with.

> So one day then
> the sun did exactly
> what the Void did;
> contemplated itself . . .

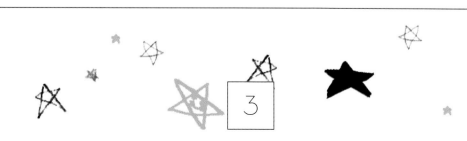

And out of itself sprang all these itsty-bitsy little suns. See them around here? Now aren't they wonderful? They have smiles; see?

Just like this guy here.

Well, he was so happy that he now had company that they all started dancing around his feet and he got very happy. And he said, "Now that I have you, we can have fun. We can do something together."

And so all the little entities sat around the feet of the sun and said, "What can we do?"

The sun said, "Let us think. What can we do?" So the sun started thinking about this and while he was thinking, he started to grow these steps . . .

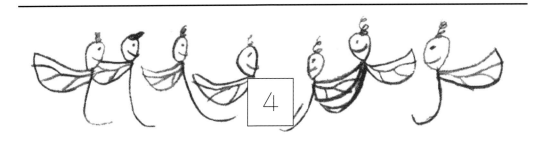

Sort of like this:

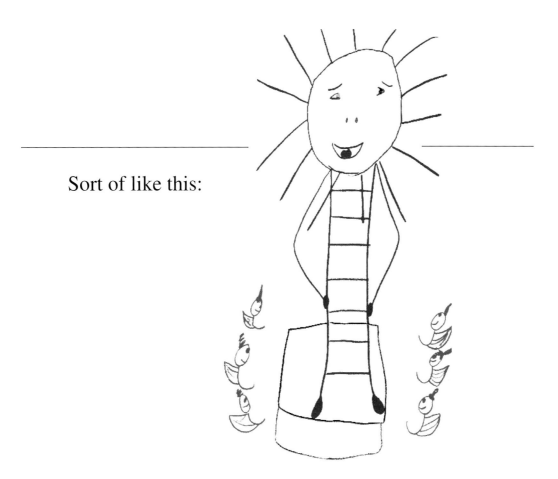

And then out of those steps he grew these legs. And to all of these little entities' amazement, the sun was changing. And they all started applauding.

And they said, "Ahh, this must be fun. Now we understand what that is".

So now God said, "Hmm. This is interesting."

And all the little entities said, "We agree. We are having fun."

And God said,

"So be it."

Now then after a little while, God said, "I've got a plan. I'm going to send all of you out to have some fun adventures."

And then they all said, "Wonderful. We are going to have fun adventures. But what pray tell is an adventure?"

And God said, "Precisely what we're all going to find out."

So then God went over there and He told them all to line up.

And remember these little beings looked like angels. And they really came out of the smiling face and rained down and became the sun's company.

So he says, "We're going to do more."

So they all lined up over here. And he says, "Now everyone who wants an adventure come up here straightaway."

So this group said, "We're going to have fun, and an adventure."

So they all lined up.

This group said, "I don't think so."

See them over here. Now see what happened to their smile? What happened here? They said, "I don't think so. We're having fun but we don't know what an adventure is."

So the sun says, "You're sure you don't want to come along?"

And they went, "We're staying with you and having fun."

So then the sun came over there and he said, "Now here's the rules. Line up. I'm going to give you something."

So each little being lined up and lo and behold the sun gave them this purple satchel.

"Purple satchel?
What is this?"

And the sun says, "This is what we're going to make an adventure out of."

So he gives it to the little entity.

Can you imagine what it is to open a bag
and nothing's in it?

See this little entity. Look, he opens up the bag,
and imagine,
"This is an adventure?
This is it?
This is all we're getting?
Can I go back over here and change my mind?"
"Once I give you the bag, that's it.
You're in for the duration."

So now, God.

Look at God.

Isn't God wonderful.

Look at those feet.

Look at those rays.

Look at that smile.

He gives one to each. And he says now, "This little bag is your treasure bag."

And they say, "Yippee. What's a treasure?"

And God said, "I am certain that we're going to find out. We're going to have an adventure. And what we collect from the adventure, you are to put in this bag."

"Got it?"

Now God says, "Now the next thing you have to do is that I want you to line up here and I want you to crawl down my belly."

"That's an adventure!"

So they all lined up and God extended his ladder
way into the Void,
so far
they couldn't
even see the bottom.

And he said, "One by one take your little bag and climb down to this ladder."

"All right, we will."

Now look at them. Which way are they looking, children? Are they looking up or down? Well, that's a clue. They're not looking back at God.

They're ready for this adventure. They're looking down, which means that's exactly where they're going.

So as they come down here, God has prepared a mall for them. You know what a mall is? So we're going shopping. They said, "This is wonderful. But what is shopping?" And God says, "Well, you get to pick anything you want out of this mall, as long as it fits."So all the little entities came down and they got the little bag.

And they're not supposed to lay it down anywhere.

They are supposed to keep it.

And they go to this very large closet . . .

. . . and we have . . . Ohhhhh!

Look at this, will you? Garments! Body garments. And
the little angels walk up and they get to pick out a body.

See those bodies hanging up there?

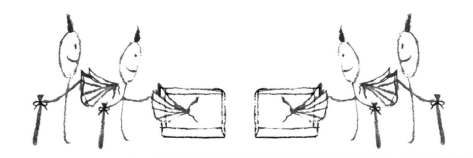

So the little entity then goes up here, picks up a body, and they get to try them all on.

See, this is fun!

Sometimes we have a little fistfight breaking out because, you see, more than one choose the purple body. And God has to make amends and make more purple bodies. And then some reject the green bodies because it doesn't look like the color of an adventure. Now they try them on and here we are; here's our little angels, come down the ladder, went shopping and now they've got on their what? Bodies? Look. How terrific this looks.

See this little entity grabbing ahold of the neck?
See this little entity here?

That is the little entity wearing this big new body that came out of this closet. And what is the entity carrying? The bag? Same bag. Now do you recognize any of these? Any of these look familiar to you? You can't tell which one of these entities chose these bodies. Do you recognize them? I don't either.

I don't know who's who.

Now isn't this wonderful.

Here they are and they're walking around in a brand new slick body that they got at God's mall.

See these guys over here?
What are they still doing?
They're not happy with any of this.

These guys have all come through and they've picked up and now they have bodies.

Wonderful.

And God looked at them and said, "You just look terrific. How does it feel?"

Well, they said, "We feel wonderful! Is this the adventure? Can we put something in the bag?"

"No, not now."

"Come on down here."

So one by one they come out of God and He said, "See this ladder? Now you're ready. I want you to walk all the way down to where this ladder ends in that new body of yours and always carry the bag, and I want you to create some adventure."

"Well, what should we do?"

"Anything you want to."

"I'll be here."

"I'll be watching."

So see this little entity is climbing down seven steps of the magic ladder to the earth. Now has he still got his bag? Still got his halo?

See the entity entering the clouds. Now who's watching up here?

These entities right here. What are they doing?

Crying oceans!

And are they waving? They're waving goodbye.

Does this entity care that they're crying?

Where is this entity looking?

Down here.

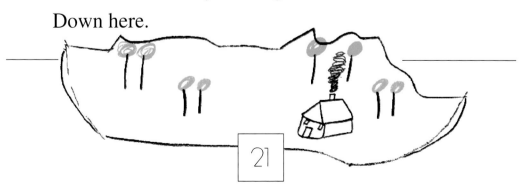

And these angels, or these other beings, they're the ones that decided not to take the journey and have the big adventure. So God said, "It's all right, you can hang around with me. And your job is to just watch this adventure." And the angel said, "Well, will we get to have what's in the little bag?"

God said, "Mmmm, I'm afraid not. That's only for those who are going to go down there and play, and your job is to help them out."

So they're crying, waving goodbye and . . .

. . . this entity is having a ball.

He's climbing down here
and suddenly now
he is building houses,
growing trees,
working for
General Motors . . .

. . . and having generally a wonderful
time. See that smoke? He's in there as we speak having
buckwheat pancakes and blueberry jam. Mmmm, that's what
the smoke is.

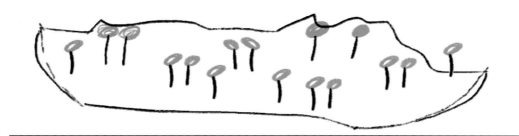

Now he's lived in this body. He's had a wonderful life. And one day he gets a stomachache. And it's probably because he ate too many buckwheat pancakes with blueberry jam. And this is after many years. And he doesn't know why, but that beautiful blue garment that he picked out at the mall, it doesn't feel as frisky as it did when he first put it on.

But of course he's done a lot since he's worn it. And he's gotten so used to it, you know, so that if he took it off, he'd feel rather naked, sort of like you do. But this one particular day, he just can't get out of bed. And he's laying there feeling bad and heavy. And suddenly before you know it . . .

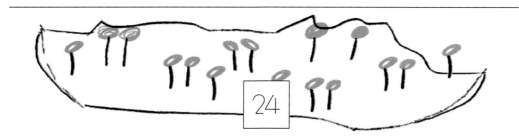

. . . he pops out of his body.

There, you see.

What's he doing? Is he smiling? Or is he . . . *smiling*?
He's happy. He's out of his body.

Now as he looks at this body, he remembers when he
went and picked it out up here.

Furthermore, children, he remembers that he used to
look like this. Happy days are here again because now he is
his old self.

So immediately he does this strange thing. He goes and sits in front of a television set. And beside the television set happens to be a being.

Now *this* being was appointed by God as one of the beings to say, "Here, now, let's see your adventure." And he turns on the television set. And the little entity standing there is watching his entire life. He watches everything!

He remembers *all the way*

when he was this little entity here.

And he saw how he ran to be first in line

And got the bag,

Was the first one to open it up,

The first one down the ladder,

The first one to yank out his body,

The first one to put it on . . .

 and look at this smile.

He remembers all of it.

Why it's as clear as day.

He remembers when he descended down the ladder to come to this place and he's watching it on this television set.

Now there's only a few things that he doesn't agree with this program.

And he starts to argue with the being.

"That isn't the way that it was."

And the being said, "Yes, it was."

"No, it wasn't."

"Yes, it was."

"No, it wasn't."

The being says, "I'm sorry, but you're wrong."

This entity says, "*I* want to go home."

The being says, "Mm-mm, no, you have to fulfill the adventure. But, you see, you're arguing with me about something that you really did do and you're in a state of denial."

And this entity says, "And what is a state of denial?"

And the being says, "Exactly what you're doing. And as long as you're doing that denial, you cannot go back up here.

And he's not going to help you. You have to get down here and make amends."

"Oh, dear."

So this little entity sits here

      And he contemplates this.

      And then he picks up a controller

      And he replays it back again.

      And he wants to see if he is in error.

      And sure enough he was in error.

      He did something wrong. Hmmm.

So as soon as he puts the controller down, he goes up to the being and says, "You're right. I was wrong.

      Can I go home?

      Please let me go home.

      Let me go back to the closet.

      I'll get a new body.

      I'll start all over.

      I'll get even a green one. How's that?"

      "No, can't do that."

      "Why?"

      "Because you're here to fulfill an adventure. You cannot go back up there and get a new body."

      "How am I gonna get one?"

      "Come with me."

So he comes over here and he says, "This is what your future life is going to look like."

And so this entity is standing here and he is watching this girl and this boy who have a strong affection for him. These are probably the two people who were right behind him.

Here, right here.

They do look familiar, don't they?

They do.

So here they are down here living it up. Isn't that wonderful? He said, "I remember you. Don't you know who I am?"

They don't even hear him. So after a while they embrace and they get one of these.

Does this look familiar?

Have you ever been one of these?

A baby; of course you have been a baby.

So he says to the being, "I have to be this? I don't want to be that. I want, I want . . . I'll be green. I don't want this, no, no. Nope, can't do it. I'll go back up."

"Nope."

"Well, what other choice do I have?"

"Come back up and watch the T.V. program over again."

"I don't want to watch my past life."

"Well, then, watch them."

"But I am bored watching them."

"Watch them."

"Why do I want to watch them?"

"Because if you are good you will grow up and look like this or maybe *this*."

So then he watches and he looks at this cute little fat thing growing and says, "Oh, my God, it's bald. I don't want to be bald. I want hair."

"You can have it."

"How much?"

"Not a lot but enough to be presentable. So be it. You can have that."

"I don't like its head. It is too big."

"It is supposed to be big."

"It looks weird."

"And why do you think it looks weird?"

"The body is so small."

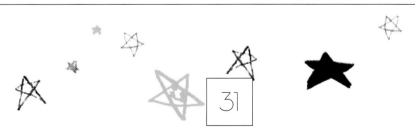

"It looks like a large melon sitting up there with hair."

"Look, if you take this and love it, I'll give it hair and it will grow tall."

"Are you sure?"

"I'm sure."

"All right, I will love it."

"So be it."

"And what about . . ."

"Yes, you are going to have your diapers changed."

"I don't . . ."

"I understand."

So anyway these two entities that he is having to watch create this unfortunate looking baby in his esteemed eyes are really rather smart. After all, they were the original group that came down here. And they had wonderful adventures over here in another part of the world. And their adventures made them very smart and very brilliant. So when they got together and started smooching it up, they created this little entity who was really better than both of them combined.

So when he realized that, he said, "Okay, I'll take it."

So then he runs and jumps into this little entity.

"Wah, wah, wah."

"Shut up."

"Wah."

Look at him. He's humiliated. He is holding onto a body that doesn't work. He knows how to make a body run, a body eat, a body laugh, a body have adventures, a body be charismatic. He knows how to pronounce the most complicated verbs.

And all this can do is,

"Wah, wah, wah."

Imagine the level of his frustration.

Knowing how to do all these with a body that can't do anything but eat and grunt. So now this must be karma.

Then he becomes the little entity, and he's holding onto that little baby for dear life.

And every once in a while his parents take a strong look at him and they start looking into his eye, into the baby's eye, and the Spirit is going like this:

Spirit gets in the way, gets right in front of the baby's face as the parents are looking at him and he's going, "*You remember me. I was first.*"

And the parents go, "Goo-goo, ga-ga, goo-goo, ga-ga. Look, Howard, he's trying to talk."

And you all did that.

And really he's thinking that his parents are going to see him . . . and he's really rather terrific.

Just like all of you did. You all did this. You looked at your mother and your father when she was holding you and he was holding you, and they were going, "*Look at those little cheeks.*" And you moved right up close to your mother and father and said, "Hey, it's me. I'm here." And you wished they would talk to you like you were there, instead of Play Dough.

But as we can see, this was their first lifetime in garments too. And they got together a little late. And they had this child. But this child was the apple of their eye. They loved this little "goo-goo, ga-ga."

And after a while the Spirit, so frustrated at not being able to make the baby's mouth talk, and every time it pointed a finger to say, "Look, Harvey, it's me." Every time it would do a finger, the finger would go up Harvey's nose.

And it would say, "*Harvey, it's me. Howard.*"
Finally the Spirit that's holding on for dear life, and all
of these entities going, "*Look, wait 'til they hear about this.*"
But he's determined.
He's going to have an adventure.
He's got this sack around his neck that he has to keep.
And suddenly he gives up.

And so when his mother says,
"There, there, there,"
he goes, "Goo-goo, ga-ga."

Because he just gives up trying to communicate and just becomes the baby. How many of you remember doing that? You remember doing that? You remember being very smart at one time and nobody knew you were, so you gave up?

Now they loved him and brought him up properly. And they did such a superb job of it that he was so brilliant because they had absolute love and affection for him. And when he finally stopped fighting and just dissolved into the baby, he grew up into this wonderful entity.

And notice he still has a purple body. He didn't have to have a green body after all. And he grew up to be so smart that he was able to figure out the most sacred laws of the universe, $E=mc^2$.

Now he was sort of a nerd in the beginning. But the Spirit, this entity here, after he was old enough to make his mouth work and his fingers point the right way and his feet move properly, then his Spirit was able to take over the body and start giving him all this knowledge.

And he didn't have to speak in some foreign language like "goo-goo, ga-ga." He could actually enunciate his thoughts with his current body.

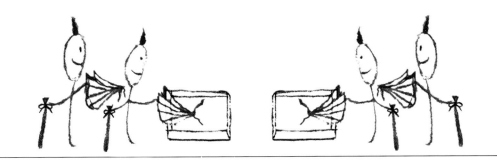

Now what happened to the purple bag? Well, remember back here when he's having to play his life over again? Remember way back here?

Remember when he left his body here? All of you did. And he went up here and he saw his life stories. Remember when he was arguing with this being that he really hadn't done some of those things that he was seeing? How many of you remember?

And the being said,
"Oh, yes, you did."
And he said,
"Oh, no, I didn't."

Well, he didn't get to put anything in his bag. He went a whole lifetime without putting anything in his bag. And it wasn't until he decided to come back down here and do it right that he finally grew up to be this. And he was so brilliant and such a leader that he did so many wonderful things to help humanity, other spiritual beings, in other garments, that when his life was over . . .

. . . Look at this.

Now he's getting to go home.
What's he got in the bag?
Treasure?
What else?
Knowledge and adventures.
Now take a look at this entity going up the ladder. Is he looking up or down? Sure he's not looking down? He's looking up because he did exactly what God told him to do.

"Here's an empty sack.
Go and have an adventure.
Make known the unknown.
And every time you do, you
get to put that in the sack.
And when it's filled up, come
back home to me and let's
create another adventure."

So be it.

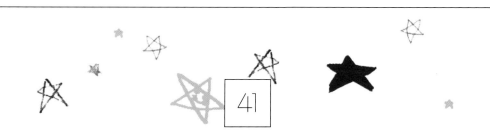

So now what I want you to know is that even though you're sort of small and the grown-ups never really look at you, sometimes that's a blessing.

Because you really don't want them to notice you.

That way you can be more of a spiritual being than being a child. And the reason I told you this story is that I already know that you're already one of these beings. It's just that before you were born into this life, you saw your parents here. And you had no other option but to come back and be born again because you haven't filled your bag with experience.

Now what is important for you to understand is that you're in a little body. But see this entity here. Your Spirit's got ahold of you. And sometimes in a little body it doesn't work the way you want it to work, as you all know.

And then there's sometimes that you, your Spirit — who you used to remember — goes to sleep. And you wake up one morning and you kind of know that because you wake up and you're a kid, a little person, a rebel. And you start acting out your body instead of your Spirit.

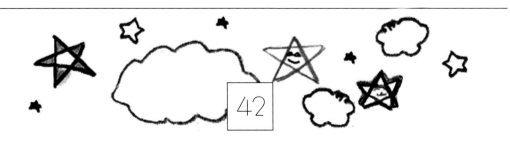

42

And what I'm here to tell you by this story is that you're not here by accident. And before you were born, you knew your parents. And that you were sent back here and you wanted to come back to them.

You wanted to come back to them because you wanted to do in this life what you did not do in the other life. The purple bag is your soul. And why you came back here is to put experiences in this bag. And the experiences can't be good experiences or bad experiences; they must be noble experiences. That means that everything you do, must be done; that no matter who sees your thought, you wouldn't be ashamed if the entire world could read it. And that everything that you do, you're proud to show everyone, including this entity here.

Now how many of you do good things so that your parents are proud of you? That is wonderful because their love and admiration goes a long way when you make it better. But you are also a child of God. And so everything you do in this lifetime, I want you to know that God is watching you and hoping that you'll be better than you were in your last lifetime.

You will be better in everything that you do. And that every once in a while you will stop being a child and remember you're a Spirit in a little person's body and that you have a destiny to fulfill.

And at the end of this life, if you fulfill that destiny, you're going to go back here and watch this television screen after you leave your body and you're going to get to see this life all over again.

As a matter of fact, one of the things that you're going to view in the future is you sitting here listening to this story.

And from this story you can say, "That night I became aware that I really was a Spirit, a child of God, in my parent's body.

And that I wanted to grow up to be godlike
and have an adventure."

And then if you approve of this life . . .

you get to take all of that . . .

and go back home.

Now, angels. Everyone
talks about angels. But angels
have never lived in a human
body. They've never lived in
a human body. Here they are.

Right here.

Angels were the same people that you were
that were seated at the feet of God. And when God
said, "Let's have an adventure," they stayed behind.

And only the brave went to do this adventure.

And because they stayed behind, they never got to go and pick out, do a little shopping, get a little purple bag, go down a golden stair step, and live in a real house. They never got to do that. All they are is a spiritual being that watches everything you do. And they will continue to watch everything you do because let me tell you what an angel thinks about you.

An angel considers children and people the bravest of them all because you did what they would not do. And they're here to help you, but it's your life. So they have profound love and respect for you because you did what they wouldn't do. Angels are not better than you. This group of beings is not better than you. They are Gods. But they will never be God-child-realized because they've never been like you.

So you come to school here to learn from me. Maybe before you came down this ladder you chose your parents because you wanted to come here and learn. And that what I was going to teach you is to remember this, that you're not really your body. You are really one of these divine beings who's been given the purple sack of adventure. And I never want you to forget it.

So be it.

Now one day you're going to be grown up. And I won't be here. And one day you're going to remember me and this story that I told you. And no matter what happens, I never want you to destroy these drawings because one day each one of you is going to be in a situation that the only help you're ever going to get is to pull this book out and to remember the story that I told you. And when you read it and remember, I'll send my help to you immediately. That's all . . .

. . . I love you.